M000045759

CREDO: I BELIEVE

CREDO: I BELIEVE

—

EDITED BY
CALEB KEITH AND KELSI KLEMBARA

Credo: I Believe

© 2019 1517 Publishing

All rights reserved. No part of this publication may be reproduced, distributed, or transmitted in any form or by any means, including photocopying, recording, or other electronic or mechanical methods, without the prior written permission of the publisher, except in the case of brief quotations embodied in critical reviews and certain other noncommercial uses permitted by copyright law. For permission requests, write to the publisher at the address below.

Unless otherwise indicated, all Scripture quotations are from The ESV® Bible (The Holy Bible, English Standard Version®), copyright © 2001 by Crossway, a publishing ministry of Good News Publishers. Used by permission. All rights reserved.

Published by:
1517 Publishing
PO Box 54032
Irvine, CA 92619-4032

Publisher's Cataloging-In-Publication Data
(Prepared by The Donohue Group, Inc.)

Names: Keith, Caleb, editor. | Klembara, Kelsi, editor.
Title: Credo : I believe / edited by Caleb Keith and Kelsi Klembara.
Description: Irvine, CA : 1517 Publishing, [2019] | Includes
    bibliographical references.
Identifiers: ISBN 9781945978784 (softcover) | ISBN 9781948969284
    (ebook)
Subjects: LCSH: Apostles' Creed—Criticism, interpretation, etc. |
    Creeds. | LCGFT: Essays.
Classification: LCC BT993.3 .C74 2019 (print) | LCC BT993.3
    (ebook) | DDC 238/.11—dc23

Printed in the United States of America

Cover art by Brenton Clarke Little.

CONTENTS

THE APOSTLES' CREED

I believe in God, the Father almighty,
maker of heaven and earth,

And in Jesus Christ, his only Son, our Lord,
who was conceived by the Holy Spirit,
born of the Virgin Mary,
suffered under Pontius Pilate,
was crucified, died and was buried.
He descended into hell.
The third day he rose again from the dead.
He ascended into heaven
and sits at the right hand of God
the Father almighty.
From there he will come to judge the living and
the dead.

I believe in the Holy Spirit,
the holy catholic church,
the communion of saints,
the forgiveness of sins,
the resurrection of the body,
and the life everlasting. Amen.

I BELIEVE

CALEB KEITH

WHAT IS A CREED?

"I believe." These two words precede conversations we have every single day. Statements of belief, no matter how small, are used to connect our personal thoughts, intentions, and actions to the world around us. While sometimes shrugged off as a mere opinion, the "I believe" of everyday life is in some way connected to facts. If I tell my wife, "I believe I put gas in the car," and on her drive to work, the car sputters and spits as it runs on empty, then my belief will not have mattered in the least. She will likely lose trust in my ability to assure her it's safe to take the car to work. For the Christian, the words "I believe" tie the individual to the reality of salvation accomplished by the death and resurrection of Jesus Christ. The statement of belief is not about mere feelings, wishing, or guessing; rather, it is a pointed statement of fact.

The development of the historical Christian creeds arose out of the struggle to clearly and concisely define the truths of Scripture and reject beliefs contrary to the gospel of Jesus Christ. Thus, the creeds became a guiding light, highlighting the essential truths revealed by the Scriptures. When people speak these truths, they are making a confession. They are personally binding and trusting themselves to its words.

Sometimes confessing is seen as a totally negative experience. The imagination is drawn to a courtroom or a Roman Catholic confessional box, where the guilty party is prepared to alleviate his or her conscience and in return, receive his or her sentence. However, in the Christian life confessing is not inherently negative. In either positive or negative form, both a confession of the faith and a confession of sin are great gifts from God.

The Christian life is one of confession—confession of true guilt and confession of true hope, as well as confession of true law and confession of true gospel. The earliest public Christian confessions of faith are referred to as creeds. Simply put, creeds are the formulation of biblical truths into public statements.

The word *creed* is derived from the Latin verb *credo*. It means, quite simply, "I believe." In its fuller sense, it is a personal declaration of trust in something or someone.

We are familiar with the trusting aspect of *credo* from the English word *credit*. When people are given credit, they are trusted with something. Sometimes that thing is money or possessions, but often it involves simple, daily exchanges. If somebody visits my home and notices how well put together it is, I would credit my wife for that accomplishment.

The credit of the Christian creeds functions in a similar way. Like a fiscal exchange, a creed entrusts its confessor with a great gift—the gift of knowledge in the faith. Like the credit of daily accomplishments, the creeds direct believers to whom the accomplishment of life and salvation belongs—namely the triune God.

The purpose of this collection of essays on the central confessions of the creeds is to approach and break down what it means to confess the core tenants of the Christian faith as outlined by the Apostles' Creed. Regardless of whether you have heard of the Apostles' Creed or not, the content of this creed, which has been confessed for over fifteen hundred years, is important to reflect on as professing Christians.

THE CHALLENGE OF TEACHING CREEDS IN CONTEMPORARY CHRISTIANITY

It is not unusual for contemporary Christians and Christian churches to reject or replace the use of the creeds. Justin Holcomb highlights this problem:

Nowadays, we have a largely literate population and an ample supply of Bibles, and so it's easy to wonder whether creeds are necessary. Some may even think that the creeds stand in opposition to (or at least in tension with) the authority of Holy Scripture.[1]

However, this opposition to the creeds misunderstands that they are not a force used to contain or limit Scripture. Instead, Holcomb continues, "creeds are themselves drawn from the Bible and provide a touchstone to the faith for Christians of all times and places."[2] The core of that touchstone is belief in the death and resurrection of Christ for the forgiveness of sins, a truth that the creeds have helped maintain

---

[1]Justin Holcomb, *Know the Creeds and Councils* (Grand Rapids, MI: Zondervan, 2014), 5.
[2]Ibid., 6.

throughout history even when teachers and preachers have forgotten it.

Christians did not invent the confessions contained in the early creeds. Rather, they were taken directly from Scripture. Scripture itself contains portions of creeds and encourages their use. Romans 10:9–10 states, "[I]f you confess with your mouth that Jesus is Lord and believe in your heart that God raised him from the dead, you will be saved. For with the heart one believes and is justified, and with the mouth one confesses and is saved." And 1 Timothy 3:16 says, "Great indeed, we confess, is the mystery of godliness: He was manifested in the flesh, vindicated by the Spirit, seen by angels, proclaimed among the nations, believed on in this world, taken up in glory."

These scriptural confessions are short and memorable, recounting the reality, purpose, and accomplishment of Christ's life and salvific work. It is all but impossible to memorize the entirety of the Bible verse by verse. It's hard to memorize just one book. Creeds allow us to condense the teachings of the Bible into a short statement so the core doctrines of Christianity can be memorized by heart. With the creeds, believers may never be without both these treasured truths, in good times as well as times of trouble and doubt.

A REFORMATION MODEL FOR TEACHING THE FAITH

Creeds as confessions of the core teachings of the Bible also help to temper the inclination to subjectively interpret the Bible or even reimagine the faith that was once delivered to the saints (Jude 1:3). During the Lutheran Reformation, Philip Melanchthon regularly used the phrase *non nova dogmata*, or "There are no new teachings!" While there is little argument that the church today looks different than it did one hundred, five hundred, and even two thousand years ago, the truth of salvation remains the same.

This is why the Lutheran Reformation was not a total upheaval. The reformers recognized that the greatest errors of the medieval Roman church were not its visual style or traditions but teachings that had been invented over the course of time. This is why, in the midst of doctrinal reform and struggle, the reformers returned to and used the creeds throughout their confessions. As Luther put it in the *Large Catechism*,

> **But the Creed, brings sheer grace; and it makes us righteous and acceptable to God. Through this knowledge we come to love and delight in all the commandments of God because we see here in the Creed how God gives himself completely to us,**

with all his gifts and power, to help us keep the Ten Commandments: the Father gives us all creation, Christ all his works, the Holy Spirit all his gifts.[3]

What I wish to steal from Luther, Melanchthon, and the Reformation is the deep concern for teaching the faith, not arbitrarily, but with urgency and fidelity to the Bible. The knowledge of faith is not cold or detached; it is comfort and rescue to poor, miserable sinners. The creeds help focus, center, and preserve the faith.

The following chapters are concerned with the most basic Christian creed—the Apostles' Creed. They seek to address two simple questions: What makes the teachings of the Apostles' Creed necessary for faith in Christ? And what does it mean to confess these things as true? My hope is that through every chapter it is made clear that the Apostles' Creed and other historical creeds are seen not as something to be avoided but as tools to help us daily die and rise with Christ so we might stand firm in faith, united to him in death and resurrection.

---

[3] *Large Catechism*, in *The Book of Concord: The Confessions of the Evangelical Lutheran Church*, ed. Robert Kolb, Timothy J. Wengert, and Charles P. Arand (Minneapolis, MN: Augsburg Fortress Publishing, 2000), 440.

IN GOD THE FATHER

SCOTT L. KEITH

From Martin Luther's *Small Catechism*:

> I believe in God the Father Almighty, Maker of heaven and earth.

What Does This Mean?

I believe that God has made me and all creatures; that He has given me my body and soul, eyes, ears, and all my limbs, my reason, and all my senses, and still preserves them; in addition thereto, clothing and shoes, meat and drink, house and homestead, wife and children, fields, cattle, and all my goods; that He provides me richly and daily with all that I need to support this body and life, protects me from all danger, and guards me and preserves me from all evil; and all this out of pure, fatherly, divine goodness and mercy, without any merit or worthiness in me; for all which I owe it to

Him to thank, praise, serve, and obey Him. This is most certainly true.[1]

This section of the *Small Catechism* is helpful when thinking about what God the Father is like. This idea often falls under what is called "First Article" or "Creation Order" concepts of doctrines of Christianity. Specifically, the First Article deals with God as Creator and Sustainer of all things—especially the earth, the heavens, and people like you and me. So the above answer to, "What does this mean?" has served as a touchpoint for countless people, especially for Christians from Reformation traditions throughout the centuries. And while the above is "most certainly true," it often leaves us still asking for more of an explanation. But maybe if we look closer at what Luther does in his explanation to the First Article, it will become clearer and seem more sufficient.

Are there any pictures of God here on the earth that can give us a glimpse into what God is like? This question is common in theological conversations, even in those informed by Luther's *Catechism*. Interestingly enough, when God refers to himself as "Father," he gives us a glimpse of himself. He does so using language that

---

[1] *Small Catechism*, in *Concordia Triglotta*, ed. F. Bente (St. Louis, MO: Concordia Publishing House, 1921), 543.

we are familiar with and often draws us into his description based on our own experiences. Luther expounds on this language in his explanation to the first article of the creed. He describes God the Father by describing those things the Father does for us and what he gives us. God the Father provides house and home, food and clothing, and all we need for this body and life. In an interesting twist, many of these are the same things good earthly fathers provide for us as well.

HOW GOD REVEALS HIMSELF

In theological terms, this is called an *analogia entis* or an analogy of being—something that provides a comparison between two proportions. The great thinker and theologian Thomas Aquinas (1225–1274) is helpful to us as we attempt to work out how God reveals himself to us. The difficulty is our inability to express or comprehend God's greatness and magnitude. Aquinas claimed that our human language, as we try to explain God, is neither univocal (using the same word in precisely the same way) nor equivocal (using the same word in different ways). Instead, as we, in our feeble way, try to discuss and understand what God is or what he is like, we use analogical language and denotative definitions. As an example, when we say, "God is good" and "A good father is good," we do not mean exactly the same thing. As the Scriptures tell it, God is good in a completely unique way—one that is, on the whole, beyond our understanding of the word *good*. Yet when we say, "a good father is good," we don't mean something that is exactly the opposite of what is meant when we say, "God is good." These two statements are meant analogically. That is, we are using an analogy to get the point across or point to something or someone—in this case, a good father.

This language is helpful for several reasons. We all tend to understand things better when definitions are given by way of example rather than when we do by mere description. So analogies can serve as pictures that we point to in order to give us a better idea of what God is like in real life. This type of definition is called denotative.

Think of it this way: pretend that you had never seen a chair, and someone is trying to describe to you, only with words, what a chair is and what it is like. They might say it is an item intended to sit upon that has four legs (sometimes fewer), a seat, and a back. They might further describe that it needs to be constructed to be strong enough to support the entire weight of your body. Your friend might also attempt to communicate that chairs can come in all sorts of different shapes and sizes, at which point you might become confused. How much easier would it be for this friend simply to take you to a place full of chairs and show you one, or several, and allow you to sit in them to check them out for yourself? Once you are shown real chairs, your confusion would likely disappear and you would, from that point on, be left with a good idea—a good picture—of what a chair is.

Analogies and denotative ways of communicating are helpful for just this reason. They give us more complete and concrete, though not perfect, pictures of complex ideas. And this is how it is with God the Father. The mere idea of him is so beyond us that we often have trouble wrapping our heads around it.

OUR FATHER'S CHARACTERISTICS

We are told that God the Father is *omnipotent* or all-powerful. That is, unlike us, he can do anything he sets his mind to do. This is most perfectly illustrated in the creation account of Genesis 1. There, the text tells us, "In the beginning, God created the heavens and the earth."

This is a phenomenal feat and would take immense power and ability to accomplish. So, how does God do this? Again, the text is helpful as it tells us that God simply says, "let there be," and out of nothing there is. This type of power is hard to imagine, unless we can point to a shadowy, though imperfect, example of similar power. Maybe it is a very powerful man, or machine, or a powerful and protective friend or earthly father. The here-and-now examples make the omnipotence of God the Father slightly easier to comprehend. Again, this is not a perfect picture of God's power, but it is concrete, tangible, understandable, and easy to connect.

We are also told that God the Father is *omniscient* or all-knowing. Here again we come to understand God the Father is so unlike us that he does not have to guess at what has happened, is happening, or will happen. He simply knows all. This is a difficult concept for us mere mortals to understand. Some of us want so badly to know more that there is an entire branch of philosophy, called epistemology, dedicated to the topic. The fact that we do not know more than we do often vexes us. Yet we can imagine what it might be like to know more or even dare to imagine what it might be like to know all.

This imagining often takes the form of comparing ourselves to someone who does know more than we do. An older, wiser person often serves as this comparison point for us. Maybe a father or mother, grandmother or grandfather, or a wise old uncle. Again, this denotative or analogical type of imagining can help make God more approachable.

We are also told that God the Father is *omnipresent*—that is, he is everywhere always. This one is very difficult for us to imagine. We don't know anyone who can be everywhere at once, do we? No, we certainly do not. But we do know people who seem to always be there for us. They appear in person, on the phone, or sometimes just in our memory right in the nick of time. They care for us and serve us at just the right time. They too provide an analogy of being like our omnipresent God the Father who is always there for us.

Finally, we are told that God the Father is *benevolent* or all-good. Everyone born into this world is born into sin and is thus *not good*. But though we are all sinful and unclean, we can in our God-given calling to others be good to people in ways we cannot even imagine. This is the idea or doctrine of vocation.

Because of all of the aforementioned attributes of God, it is clear to his children that he does not actually need things from them and that quite the reverse is true: we need all things from him. Thus, we pray things like, "Give us this day our daily bread." Yet when he answers this prayer, he answers through other people, other sinners, like us. Other people grow the food, harvest it, transport it, and store it. Eventually, through grocery stores or restaurants, it ends up with us. This is vocation. Through our vocations, we serve others and are good to others even when we do not realize we are. By understanding how God works through vocation, we can see little shadows of God's goodness everywhere and know better what it means when we say, "God is good."

So, to wrap this up, we see that God the Father is good, that he knows all of our needs and has the power, presence, and desire to fulfill them for us. He is not omniscient, omnipotent, omnipresent, or benevolent simply for the sake of being those things. He is all-knowing, powerful, present, and good for our sake. He places people in our lives to serve us in their vocations, and in so doing, his love showers over us. Of course, these people who serve us are shadowy and imperfect reflections of what God the Father is really like. We must admit, however, that it is easier for us to believe in a God who is among us than one who is apart from us. God the Father is often presented in a way where he seems far away from us when in fact he is right there beside us through the little analogies of being we call the fellowship of the saints. He is near to us through those neighbors we interact with day after day.

So, in answer to the question we originally asked, "Are there any pictures of God here on the earth that can give us a glimpse into what God is like?" we answer, I hope, in one resounding voice, "Yes, there are millions of them, and they are all around us." Certainly, some of the clearest examples of this are good fathers in the lives of their children, but we could also point out good mothers, friends, grandfathers and grandmothers, wise old uncles, mentors and teachers, and so on. Anyone who provides for us freely, cares for us freely, protects us without question, is there for us when we need help, and loves us, points us to a picture of God the Father. Those who supply what we need through their vocations are also glimpses of God.

What is left then? Merely to thank and praise him for giving his First Article and Creation Order goodness to us daily, even though there isn't any merit or worthiness within us. Yet, his love showers upon us by miraculous and common means every single day! This is the work of God the Father, and this is most certainly true.

IN JESUS CHRIST HIS SON

DANIEL EMERY PRICE

Too often we view the Old Testament as the part of Scripture full of nothing but commands, violence, and wrath. Those things are certainly there, but they are not meant to eclipse the primary word God speaks—a word of promise. This promise was first spoken as Adam and Eve were about to be exiled from Eden (Gen. 3:15)—the promise that a Son will be born and, at significant cost to himself, will tread the devil and death under his feet. This promise was spoken again to Abraham when God vowed to bless all nations in his seed (Gen. 22:17–18). This promise was foreshadowed in Noah escaping the flood with his family in an ark and the exodus of Israel from Egypt. Generation after generation waited in anticipation for the consummation of this promise. As they waited, God reaffirmed his promise through the mouths of the prophets. God regularly followed words of rebuke and judgment by doubling down on all he had promised. One anointed by God to save the world was still going to come. That is what this article of the Apostles' Creed is about.

I BELIEVE IN THE GOD-MAN

There is nothing unique or saving about believing that Jesus existed. Most people do. Religions outside of Christianity do. The question is, what do we believe about him? Who do we confess he is? Is he simply a historical figure? The instigator of a political rebellion? A prophet who was martyred?

When we confess that Jesus is the only Son of God, we are confessing that he is God. He is the second person of the Trinity, distinct from the Father and Holy Spirit. Yet, Jesus is both the Son of God and the son of Mary. He is both human and divine. He is wholly, equally, and uniquely God and man. However, the Son of God did not find his beginning in the womb of his virgin mother. The incarnation was God revealing to the world who his only Son had always been and forever will be.

One of the primary identities of Jesus is the *Lamb of God*. When John the Baptizer saw Jesus approaching him at the Jordan River, he exclaimed, "Behold, the Lamb of God, who takes away the sin of the world!" (John 1:29). This is indeed who Jesus was (and is), but it is also who he has always been. Jesus is "the Lamb who was slain from the creation of the world" (Rev. 13:8 NIV). This is the Jesus we are confessing to believe in: the Jesus who has always been because he is God and at the same time, a man. He is God who "became flesh and made his dwelling among us" (John 1:14 NIV). We are not confessing to believe in a mere man in history, a prophet, teacher, or revolutionary. We believe in Jesus the God-Man, the Lamb of God who came to take away the sin of the whole world.

I BELIEVE JESUS IS THE CHRIST

> He (Jesus) asked his disciples, "Who do people say that the Son of Man is?" And they said, "Some say John the Baptist, others say Elijah, and others Jeremiah or one of the prophets." He said to them, "But who do you say that I am?" Simon Peter replied, "You are the Christ, the Son of the living God." (Matt. 16:13–16)

What was Peter saying when he said, "You are the Christ, the Son of the living God"? Christ comes from the Greek word *Christos*, a translation of the Hebrew title *Mashiach* (or Messiah), which means "anointed one." Peter does not declare Jesus to be a Christ but the

Christ—the definitive and final fulfillment of what God had long spoken. He is the promise who was continually on the lips of the prophets. To say Jesus is the Christ is to confess he is the Messiah vowed to Israel—the anointed one who would deliver them and the world from sin.

When we confess we believe in Jesus Christ, we are saying we believe in Jesus the anointed one. But anointed for what? To be anointed is to be chosen by God. Jesus is and has always been God's chosen answer for sin. He is the anointed Lamb of God who came to assume all sin to himself. He was chosen by God to become the sin of the world and to gift that world with his divine righteousness. He was chosen to die under the law and then rise again, and in doing so, forever defeat sin, death, and hell. As we confess Jesus to be the Christ, we confess that God has chosen him to be simultaneously where all our sin resides and the source of all our righteousness. "God made him who had no sin to be sin for us, so that in him we might become the righteousness of God" (2 Cor. 5:21 NIV).

I BELIEVE JESUS IS OUR LORD

"Fear not: for, behold, I bring you good tidings of great joy, which shall be to all people. For unto you is born this day in the city of David a Savior, which is Christ the Lord" (Luke 2:10–11 KJV).

I have often heard it said, "Jesus will not be your Savior if you will not make him your Lord." This is commonly referred to as lordship salvation. This doctrine states that the sinner must submit to the lordship of Jesus to be forgiven and redeemed. There are many theological problems with this idea. Chief among them is that Jesus did not ask us if we would like him to be our Savior and Lord. These are not things he put forward as offers for sinner subjects to accept. Our Savior and our Lord are who Jesus is. And even more than that, they are who he is *for us*.

When an angel announced the birth of Jesus to shepherds in the hills of Bethlehem, it proclaimed that what was spoken by the Prophet Isaiah had been fulfilled. "For to us a child is born, to us a son is given" (Isa. 9:6a). The angel stated that this was a good message and cause for great joy for everyone. This was good and joyful news because it was upside-down. Lords are given titles, lands, and people. A Lord is a master. However, this Lord was *given* to us. This savior was born *unto* us. This master is the servant of sinners. "The Son of Man did not come to be served, but to serve, and to give his life as a ransom for many" (Matt. 20:28).

The Apostles' Creed does not say that Jesus Christ is *the* Lord, but that he is *our* Lord. He certainly is *the*

Lord, but there is little comfort in that truth for sinners. Great comfort and joy are found when we agree with the heavenly host that Jesus Christ belongs to sinners and sinners belong to him. The John 3:16 good news is that God has given his only Son to us—that *our* Savior is Christ the Lord.

Martin Luther put it this way: "Let this be the summary of this article, that the little word 'Lord' simply means the same as Redeemer, that is, He who has brought us from the Devil to God, from death to life, from sin to righteousness, and now keeps us safe there."[1] Luther believed comfort is found in the safety of Christ's righteousness.

In great joy, we confess that Jesus Christ is our Lord. He came down from heaven for us. He came to do battle with sin, death, and the devil on our behalf. And he won. He has redeemed the world and granted its inhabitants entrance into his kingdom. The Savior of the world is our Lord.

---

[1]Martin Luther, *The Large Catechism*, trans. By Robert H. Fischer (Minneapolis: Fortress Press, 1959), 58.

I BELIEVE GOD KEEPS
HIS PROMISES

"For no matter how many promises God has made, they are 'Yes' in Christ" (2 Cor. 1:20a NIV).

To believe that Jesus is the Christ, the only Son of the Father and our Lord, is to believe that God, in Christ, has kept his promises. The promise to redeem and forgive you. The promise to justify, sanctify, and glorify you. The promise to give you eternal life. The promise to hold fast to you until all he has said is accomplished. The promise of a Son made in the garden of Eden. The promise made to Abraham of a seed in whom all nations would be blessed. The promises spoken over and over through the Old Testament prophets. To confess this article of the creed is to confess that God has not lied, that God is for us and not against us, and that salvation has come to a sinful and rebellious world just as he promised.

WHO SUFFERED AND WAS BURIED

PHILIP BARTELT

When we confess Christ's crucifixion through the phrase, "He suffered under Pontius Pilot, was crucified, died, and was buried," we confess nothing short of foolishness according to the ways of the world. As Paul states, "For the word of the cross is folly to those who are perishing, but to us who are being saved it is the power of God. . . . For Jews demand signs and Greeks seek wisdom, but we preach Christ crucified, a stumbling block to Jews and folly to Gentiles" (1 Cor. 1:18, 22–23). Even so, as Martin Luther put it, *crux sola est nostra theologia* or "the cross alone is our theology," for it is belief in the act of Christ's crucifixion, or the word of the cross, that makes true theologians.[1]

---

[1]Martin Luther, *D. Martin Luthers Werke: Kritische Gesamtausgabe*, vol. 5 (Weimar: Böhlau, 1892), 176.

CAUGHT *IN* THE ACT OF THE CROSS

Gerhard Forde defines the word of the cross as a speech act in which we are both "caught *in* the act," declared guilty, and "caught *by* the act," declared righteous.[2] When preached, the crucifixion becomes a living word, killing us and making us alive. The idea of being "caught" both by the law and the gospel is offensive as it takes all the control out of our hands and puts it into the hands of Christ, who does the "catching." Jesus came preaching repentance and the forgiveness of sins for all who believe, and we wouldn't have any of it. This rebellion is the result of what Luther names our inner theologian of glory. In contrast to a theologian of the cross, the theologian of glory is given to the wisdom and power of the world, which runs in direct opposition to the wisdom and power of God found in the cross alone.

Unfortunately, the natural man is born a theologian of glory. From the womb, the language we speak is the language of glory and power. "Behold I was brought forth in iniquity, and in sin did my mother conceive me" (Ps. 51:5). We see this plainly in the birth narrative of the patriarch Jacob the "Grabber"—so

---

[2]Gerhard O. Forde, *A More Radical Gospel,* ed. Mark C. Mattes and Steven D. Paulson (Grand Rapids, MI: William B. Eerdmans Publishing, 2004), 86–90.

named because even in the womb he wrestled with his brother and was caught grabbing his brother's ankle at birth in an attempt to claim the right as firstborn. Paul paints quite the contrast in the "Christ Hymn" where he claims that Jesus "who, though he was in the form of God, did not count equality with God a thing to be grasped, but emptied himself, by taking the form of a servant, being born in the likeness of men. And being found in human form, he humbled himself by becoming obedient to the point of death, even death on a cross" (Phil. 2:6–8).

In the eyes of the world, there is no power to be seen in the cross. There is no glory visible in the lashed and pierced body of Christ. The greatest minds in the history of the world cannot make sense of the cross. According to their reason, it is nothing short of idiocy to think God could be man, much less that God could suffer.[3] But the word of the cross stands in opposition to both mythology and metaphysics. The mythology and metaphysics of the ancients and the world's religions place God in the realm of theory and speculation. The word of the cross has God suffering and dying in history.

---

[3]Oswald Bayer, *Theology the Lutheran Way* (Minneapolis, MN: Fortress Press, 2017), 3–8.

NOT JUST A STORY, A REAL CROSS

In light of this, the confession of the word of the cross "under Pontius Pilate" is definitive for the theologian of the cross. This confession forces us to fix our eyes not somewhere "a long time ago" in a place "far, far away" but precisely on the cross in its historical and spatial dimension. In the cross, God has taken on human flesh as true man, and he has broken into real space and time to do a single thing—to rescue an entire world of sinners.

This unique historical event has far-reaching implications. The word of the cross speaks to us today. That is, the Scriptures that preach the word of the cross are not merely dead words on a page listing historical facts. These words are a hammer that shatters rock (Jer. 23). They are also the words that lift up and give life (1 Sam. 2). They are words that are living and active, sharper than any two-edged sword, piercing to the division of soul and spirit (Heb. 4).

Thus, the hearer of the word is not in the position of primacy over the text as he or she reads. Rather, it is Scripture that establishes itself as authoritative and actively makes a claim about the hearer. This is what we mean by *scriptura sacra sui ipsius interpres* or "Holy Scripture is its own interpreter." Before we turn to our own imagination to interpret a difficult text, we first turn to more clear sections of Scripture. As sinful creatures, we do not have the authority to speak over the text, rather, the word is the one that interprets the hearer. Scripture is not simply a descriptive story, but it is a declaration over the hearer that changes their reality. It is an inspired word, and as such, no one can escape Holy Scripture and the declarative word of the cross unscathed.[4]

CAUGHT *BY* THE ACT OF THE CROSS

It is at the cross that we are confronted with the truth that we are real sinners in need of a real Savior to show real mercy. However, by nature, we are theologians of glory attempting to deal abstractly with "salvation" and "mercy." But when we are actually put face-to-face with an incarnate God who comes to show mercy, we are exposed for who we really are! The only solution is for God to free us through the very real sacrifice of his Son on the cross. This is what it means for us to be caught up *by* the cross of Christ. Here, Paul's words in Galatians come like the rolling thunder of the gospel: "When the fullness of time had come, God sent forth his Son, born of woman, born under the law, to redeem those who

---

[4]Forde, *A More Radical Gospel*, 70–72.

were under the law, so that we might receive adoption as sons" (Gal. 4:4–5).

We were in need of mercy, and at just the right time God gave us mercy. That mercy is a pure gift and action of God and the cross, not a merit earned by sinners. It is precisely in his death at the hands of sinners that he rescued us from ourselves. We esteemed him stricken, smitten by God, and afflicted, but instead of allowing us to bear our sins, God laid on Jesus the iniquity of us all (Isa. 53). Out of the unspeakable love of God, the Father looked to the Son and said, "Behold I am doing a new thing! It's time to have mercy." Luther wrote,

> **When the merciful Father saw that we were being oppressed through the Law, that we were being held under a curse, and that we could not be liberated from it by anything, he sent his Son into the world, heaped all the sins of all men upon him and said to him: "Be Peter the denier; Paul the persecutor, blasphemer, and assaulter; David the adulterer; the sinner who ate the apple in Paradise; the thief on the cross. In short, be the person of all men, the one who has committed the sins of all men. And see to it that You make satisfaction for them."[5]**

[5]Martin Luther, *Luther's Works*, vol. 26 (Saint Louis, MO: Concordia Publishing House, 1963), 280.

While we were dead in our trespass, Christ took up our sin on the cross, suffered the accusation of the law, and paid the penalty for sin, which is death in our place (Rom. 5:8). Christ took everything that is ours so he could give us everything that is his.

This is the joyous exchange in which we are caught up by the cross. On account of Christ we are no longer slaves, but free (John 8:36); no longer drowning in sins, but steeped in righteousness; no longer children of wrath, but children of God (Gal. 4:7). Not only were our sin and death taken up by Christ, but they were also destroyed in his body. The sin of the world could not overcome the perfect Son of God. Nor could the law make any claim against the righteousness of Christ. Nor could Satan stand as master over the Lord of All.

Christ is the victor over all. In light of this, we can confess with Paul, "Death, where is your sting? O Death, where is your victory?" In Christ, God has beautifully adorned us in his righteousness and life as his holy bride. God does not address us sternly anymore, but as a lover promising, "I am my beloved's and my beloved is mine" (Eph. 5:25–26).[6] Thus the word of the cross declares and then interprets the Christian as one claimed and rescued by Christ.[7]

---

[6] *Luther's Works*, 31:352.
[7] *Luther's Works*, 31:347–48.

By faith we receive all these benefits, and it is only by faith we confess the word of the cross. Jesus Christ, our Lord, suffered and was crucified, killed, and buried *for you and me*. This word is truly folly to those who are perishing, but to those of us who believe, it is the power of God unto salvation (Rom. 1:17). God has undermined the wisdom of this world so that salvation comes through no other way than faith in the word of the cross. He makes us all theologians of the cross by the power of his word, which kills us to make us alive so that we might live under him in his kingdom in everlasting righteousness, innocence, and blessedness.[8]

---

[8] "The Small Catechism," in *The Book of Concord: The Confessions of the Evangelical Lutheran Church*, ed. T.G. Tappert (Philadelphia: Mühlenberg Press, 1959), 345.

ON THE THIRD DAY HE ROSE

ADAM FRANCISCO

At the center of the Apostles' Creed stands the assertion that, three days after his death, Jesus rose from the dead. For those first Christians—and the one, holy, catholic church ever since—this all happened in real time and real space—in the middle of the Hebrew month of Nisan just outside of Jerusalem in the Roman province of Judea when Pontius Pilate was prefect and Tiberius Caesar was emperor.

This doctrine (of the resurrection) is, according to St. Paul, a matter of "first importance" (1 Cor. 15:3), for the whole truthfulness of Christianity hangs on it. "If Christ has not been raised, then our preaching is in vain and your faith is in vain . . . your faith is futile and you are still in your sins" (1 Cor. 15:14, 17). It is no wonder, then, that so many of Christianity's foes have tried to undermine it in one way or another.

FABRICATION OR FACT?

It started at the very beginning. As the good news of Jesus' resurrection began to spread, the soldiers who stood watch over the tomb were paid to circulate fake news that the disciples had stolen his body and fabricated the story of his postmortem appearances (Matt. 28:11–15). In anticipation of claims like this or skepticism generally, the authors of the New Testament appealed to eyewitnesses to substantiate their claims. Paul even added a list of them to what is most likely the earliest formulation of a Christian creed ("that Christ died for our sins . . . that he was buried, that he was raised on the third day"). "He appeared to Cephas [i.e., Peter], then to the twelve. . . . Then he appeared to James, then to all of the apostles. Last of all . . . he appeared also to me" (1 Cor. 15:3–8).

In our own day and age, attacks on the resurrection are more often than not based on an assumption (made fashionable by David Hume in the eighteenth century) that miracles are impossible. This presupposition is even found in textbooks on the New Testament. For example, in Bart Ehrman's *The New Testament: A Historical Introduction to the Early Christian Writings*, an excursus explaining to his readers what they should make of the abundant descriptions of miracles in the

Bible explains that, because they are so improbable or "infinitesimally remote," they should be regarded as "impossible."[1] The descriptions of the resurrection in the gospels and the claims that it happened by the other New Testament authors should be taken as stories early Christians invented to provide meaning to their community but not real historical events.

Those who were there, whose very lives would be cut short by Roman persecutors for making such claims, insisted otherwise. "We did not follow cleverly devised myths," wrote the author of 2 Peter (1:16). They saw it with their own eyes and touched the risen Jesus with their own hands, John added (1 John 1:1). If it was a myth that the writers of the gospels were trying to pass off as real, they would not have reported it the way they did. Mary Magdalene would not be named as the first eyewitness in a culture that regarded women's testimony as questionable and inadmissible in a court of law (John 20:11–18). Paul would not have been so specific as to suggest you could interview eyewitnesses because they were still alive when he wrote his first letter to the Corinthians. And he would not have had the audacity

---

[1]Bart Ehrman, *The New Testament: A Historical Introduction to the Early Christian Writings,* fourth ed. (New York: Oxford University Press, 2008), 240.

to refer to the resurrection as a public event when he stood on trial before King Herod Agrippa in Acts 26.

Given the weight of the evidence, some contemporary skeptics have acknowledged that the earliest Christians really did believe they saw the risen Jesus. What they witnessed, though, was the result of mass hallucinations. Richard Carrier, for example, writes, "I believe the best explanation, consistent with scientific findings and the surviving evidence . . . is that the first Christians experienced hallucinations of the risen Christ, of one form or another."[2] This is desperate given the number of eyewitnesses. Gary Collins writes,

Hallucinations are individual occurrences. By their very nature only one person can see a given hallucination at a time. They certainly aren't something which can be seen by a group of people. Neither is it possible that one person could somehow induce a hallucination in somebody else. Since a hallucination exists only in the subjective, personal sense, it is obvious that others cannot witness it.[3]

[2]Richard C. Carrier, "The Spiritual Body of Christ and the Legend of the Empty Tomb," in *The Empty Tomb,* ed. Robert M. Price and Jeffrey Jaw Lowder (Amherst, NY: Prometheus, 2005), 234.

[3]Cited in Lee Strobel, *The Case for the Real Jesus* (Grand Rapids, MI: Zondervan, 2007), 143.

Other modern critics have suggested even more fatuous explanations by reviving old arguments claiming the resurrection narratives of the gospels were simply copied from mythologies about dying and rising gods found in the mystery religions of antiquity. The allegation goes something like this: "There is nothing the Jesus of the Gospels either said or did . . . that cannot be shown to have originated thousands of years before, in Egyptian Mystery rites and other sacred liturgies."[4] That is, the death and resurrection of Jesus—the central events of the gospels and the Christian faith—are "a product of Paganism!"[5] As common as they are, it is hard to take such claims seriously. To be sure, there are similarities. The ancient Persian myth of Mithras comes the closest. Its origins are very old. By the time it made its way westward and attracted a following in the Roman Empire, the god Mithras was said to have been born of a virgin on December 25, who had twelve disciples, eventually sacrificed himself, but rose three days after his death. Scholars have shown, however, that these details did not make their way into

---

[4]Tom Harpur, *The Pagan Christ* (New York: Walker & Company, 2004), 10.
[5]Timothy Freke and Peter Gandy, *The Jesus Mysteries: Was the "Original Jesus" a Pagan God?* (New York: Three Rivers Press, 1999), 9.

the stories people told about Mithras "until the mid-second century." That's well after the gospels were written.[6] It is more likely, then, that second-century Roman Mithraism was influenced by Christian ideas. All in all, there is "no *prima facie* evidence that the death and resurrection of Jesus is a mythological construct, drawing on the myths and rites of the dying and risings gods of the surrounding world."[7]

All other attempts to critique or explain away the resurrection are just as pathetic.[8] Time and again, the resurrection is shown to be, beyond a reasonable doubt, the best explanation for the empty tomb. A real historical, bodily resurrection, then, is a fact. And it's a fact that "has given assurance to all" (Acts 17:31) or as the NASB puts it, "furnished proof to all men" that the gospel is true. This is how Jesus viewed it. When he was pressed for a sign or proof of his authority, he appealed to the sign of Jonah in the synoptic gospels

---

[6]Edwin Yamauchi, *Persia and the Bible* (Grand Rapids, MI: Baker, 1996), 510.

[7]Tryggve N. D. Mettinger, *The Riddle of Resurrection: "Dying and Rising Gods" in the Ancient Near East* (Stockholm: Almqvist & Wicksell, 2001), 221.

[8]See John J. Bombaro and Adam S. Francisco, *The Resurrection Fact: Responding to Modern Critics* (Irvine, CA: New Reformation Publications, 2016).

(Matt. 12:38–42, Mark 8:11–12, Luke 11:29–30), and in John he answered challenges to his authority by saying,

"Destroy this temple, and in three days I will raise it up." The Jews then said, "It has taken forty-six years to build this temple, and will you raise it up in three days?" But he was speaking about the temple of his body. When therefore he was raised from the dead, his disciples remembered that he had said this, and they believed the Scripture and the word that Jesus had spoken. (John 2:18–22)

THE WEIGHT OF THE RESURRECTION

The resurrection isn't just about proving the gospel true or vindicating the claims of Jesus, though. It's much more than that. The resurrection means the good news isn't just a good story, but rather it is the best story anyone could hear, for by it we are justified. As Paul wrote, Jesus "was delivered up for our trespasses and raised for our justification" (Rom. 4:25), and those who confess and believe that "God raised him from the dead . . . will be saved" (Rom. 10:9).

Our salvation from sin and death is contingent upon it. First Corinthians 15:17–19 reads: "If Christ has not been raised, your faith is futile and you are still in your sins. Then those also who have fallen asleep in Christ have perished. If in Christ we have hope in this life only, we are of all people most to be pitied." But he did rise! Or, continuing on, Paul writes, "*In fact* Christ has been raised from the dead." In doing so, he was "the firstfruits" of those who have died. "For as by a man came death, by a man has come also the resurrection of the dead. For as in Adam all die, so also in Christ shall all be made alive." Christ was the first. At his second coming, both the living and the dead "who belong to Christ" will follow. Then will come the end "where the last enemy to be destroyed is death." (1 Cor. 15:20–26).

All this—forgiveness, justification, and life everlasting —accomplished by Christ's resurrection might seem too good to be true, and it would be if Jesus did not rise. Yet he did. History bears witness to this. It is what we bear witness to when we confess that three days after his crucifixion and death, he rose again from the dead. This is not the only fact we confess, however. We bear witness to Christ's triumph over sin and death, by which we are the chief beneficiaries. Our sins are forgiven. We are made right before God. We stand confident that, at the last day, we will be raised to newness of life.

While our confession of the resurrection is an assertion about what happened in the past, it is likewise a confession of what that event means for us—that our justification is an accomplished fact. When we confess that, after three days, Christ rose again, we also confess and look forward to our own resurrection (Rom. 6:4–10). And we can stand, assured of our salvation, and boldly claim: "Death is swallowed up in victory. O death, where is your victory? O death, where is your sting? . . . Thanks be to God, who gives us the victory through our Lord Jesus Christ" (1 Cor. 15:54–57).

IN THE HOLY SPIRIT

CALEB KEITH

As you read through the words of the Apostles' Creed, you might notice that the Holy Spirit is mentioned twice—once, in direct relationship to the incarnation of Jesus Christ, and a second time, standing guard to the Holy Catholic Church, the communion of saints, and the resurrection of the dead. The creed makes abundantly clear that the Holy Spirit is not a side character in the story of redemption; he is present from start to finish. However, the visibility and action of the Spirit can be warped by imaginative stereotypes of ghosts, premonitions, and unexplained feelings, or conversely, suspicion or skepticism of anything spiritual. As philosophical presuppositions and pop culture trickle their way into doctrinal literature on the Holy Spirit, beliefs concerning the third person of the trinity can fall toward dramatic opposites in either charismatic, new-age infatuation, on the one hand, or complete disregard for the work and person of the Holy Spirit, on the other. In this chapter, I am not seeking to craft a sort of philosophical middle ground between these two camps as an attempt at bringing the best of both worlds together. Instead, just as the Apostles' Creed confesses, my aim is to boldly declare, alongside the Scriptures, that God has given all Christians his Spirit so we might hear, receive, and cling to the gospel of Christ.

The doctrine of the Holy Spirit has at times been turned into an abstraction. The word *spirit* conjures up the ethereal and intrinsically points the mind away from physicality. However, when it comes to the work of the Spirit, this instinct is not totally correct. The life presented by the giver of life in this world and the next is physical. This is not to say that the Holy Spirit is not spiritual or that he does not act in a spiritual manner but that spiritual and physical things are not as binary as we might think. From Scripture, we confess that the Spirit is constantly present and directing the interactions between the spiritual and the physical.[1] The Spirit turns what otherwise might be endless searching and pondering into concrete comfort. His movement is not exclusively personal or emotional; it is part of the salvific act of moving creatures from death to sin to life in Christ.

Confessing the Spirit is not about receiving an abundance of internal signs. Instead, we confess belief

---

[1] Genesis 1:2, Psalm 104:30, Luke 1:35.

in the Holy Spirit by trusting in his external gifts that breathe life to us, personally. This is attested to in 1 Corinthians 12:13, where Paul writes, "For in one Spirit we were all baptized into one body—Jews or Greeks, slaves or free—and all were made to drink of one Spirit." The Spirit creates, renews, and marks the church not mysteriously but through identifiable promises and established means. These means were named by the Reformers as those things that make up the church.[2]

THE SPIRIT AND THE WORD

The third person of the Trinity is an enabler. He takes otherwise ordinary and spiritually stagnant things and uses them to breathe life into a dead creation. This quite literally starts with breath as we talk about the Spirit working through the means of transmitted words. When God uses words, they are not merely descriptive but creative. In other words, when God speaks, action happens. His words are efficacious. This is evident in the very first lines of Genesis. "And God said, 'Let there be light, and there was light'" (Gen. 1:3).

But this efficacious power doesn't stop at the initial creative act. Throughout the entirety of Scripture, God

---

[2]"The Augsburg Confession," in *The Book of Concord*, 43.

continues to use his word to cause action. When God speaks his word of law, the sinner is convicted of sin. The conviction of the law and the death it causes is neither ethereal nor allegorical (1 Cor. 15:56). It is a real and physical part of life that we daily observe and experience. In the same way, when God speaks his word of gospel, his words are not an airy description of life but rather a creative statement that brings real physical life through resurrection. This new life is wrought by the Holy Spirit through Christ's incarnation, which C.S. Lewis aptly described as "The central miracle asserted by Christians."[3] At the incarnation, the word—something totally intangible—embraces and takes on humanity in its full physical and bodily reality. It is life, secured by the Holy Spirit through baptism, which will be fulfilled through the bodily resurrection of the dead. Therefore, when we confess belief in the Holy Spirit, we confess that, by the Holy Spirit, God's active word creates our faith not as simply a good idea but as a secured reality.

Like the cross of Christ, God once again gets his hands dirty in the work of the Spirit. The working out of salvation stands incomplete without the work of all three persons of the Trinity. The Father's benevolence

---

[3]C.S. Lewis, *The Joyful Christian: 127 Readings* (New York: Collier Books, 1984), 52.

and Christ's atoning work do not stand idle, but they are delivered to the sinner by the Spirit, who creates and renews faith through water, word, bread, and wine. He does not stay distant but goes straight for the heart. As Melanchthon states, "In a word, grace is nothing but the forgiveness and remission of sins; the gifts the Holy Spirit who regenerates and sanctifies the heart."[4] By the work of the Holy Spirt, we do not see God only working in the past tense but actively here and now "for you."[5]

When the scriptural promises of where the Holy Spirit is present and works are underemphasized or ignored altogether, the temptation arises to fill the gaps with our own works. Without assurance in the outward gifts of the Holy Spirit, the only place to turn is inward—to one's own works, feelings, or emotions—as a litmus test for salvation. Luther provides a balanced voice in response to either of these extremes in his commentary on Galatians 5 and the fruit of the Spirit. His approach bridges the gap between the emotive and personal effects of the Spirit and the promised external work:

---

[4]Philip Melanchthon, *The Loci Communes of Philip Melanchthon*, *ed.* C. Hill and E. Flack (Eugene, OR: Wipf & Stock, 2007), 171.

[5]Gerhard O. Forde, *Theology is for Proclamation* (Minneapolis, MN: Fortress Press,1990), 29.

Instead, when we hear the external word, we receive a certain fervor and internal light by which we are moved to exist as new creatures. In the same way, we also receive a new way to judge a new feeling, and new emotions. This change and this new judgement is due not to the work of reason or the power of man, but is the gift and the workings of the Holy Spirit that comes with the preaching of the Word that purifies our hearts through faith and awakens in us a new spiritual motive.[6]

Notice Luther states these new emotions are not spontaneous, nor are they signs unto themselves. Instead, they are wholly spoken of as resulting from the external action of the Spirit through the preached word.

The Spirit brings faith and assurance in which the believer can rely on the experience of Christ rather than personal inner experience tainted by sin. Luther writes, "In these matters, which concern the spoken, external Word, it must be firmly maintained that God gives no one his Spirit or grace apart from the external Word."[7] Thus, the Holy Spirit is not something we must dig down deeper within ourselves to find; he is present

---

[6]Luther, *Martin Luther's Commentary on Saint Paul's Epistle to the Galatians (1535)*, trans. Haroldo S. Camacho (Irvine, CA: 1517 Publishing, 2018), 328.

[7]"The Smalcald Articles," in *The Book of Concord*, 322.

and gifted through the external and physical means of God's efficacious word. To deliver this faith to us, the Spirit uses fellow sinful creatures who preach to us, drown us in the waters of baptism, and serve us Christ's body and blood.

In the *Heidelberg Disputation*, Luther describes the vocations of Christians as the rusty and jagged tools that God, the perfect craftsman, uses to complete his work.[8] This is a great comfort since as tools, we are not burdened with the task of creating new ways to interact with God, but instead he makes a promise to continually come and work through us in baptism, the Lord's Supper, and proclamation of the word.[9] By this *extra nos* (outside of us) work, the Spirit changes and brings us to new experiences *in nobis* (inside of us).

The human creature is not totally perfected in this life. It retains the desire to take the Spirit's gifts and claim them as merit.[10] As Paulson warns, "We do not

---

[8]Caleb Keith and Kelsi Klembara, *Theology of the Cross: Luther's Heidelberg Disputation and Reflections on Its 28 Theses* (Irvine, CA: 1517 Publishing, 2018), 16.

[9]First Corinthians 12:13, "For in one Spirit we were all baptized into one body." First Corinthians 11:26, "For as often as you eat this bread and drink the cup, you proclaim the Lord's death until he comes." Romans 10:17, "So faith comes from hearing, and hearing through the word of Christ."

[10]"The Formula of Concord: Solid Declaration," in *The Book of Concord*, 588.

want God to be one, unique, and to act so potently that it leaves no room for humans to fill a gap, contribute, or have at least a little potential or power."[11] However, the doctrine of the Holy Spirit is precisely a guard against such self-justification, emphasizing that such experience is not salvation itself but rather the fruits of salvation. Thus, in Galatians 5:22–24 Paul writes, "But the fruit of the Spirit is love, joy, peace, patience, kindness, goodness, faithfulness, gentleness, self-control; against such things there is no law. And those who belong to Christ Jesus have crucified the flesh with its passions and desires."

Returning to the Apostles' Creed, we confess that the Holy Spirit is not hidden but stands in plain sight, delivering Christ to us so we may believe and be moved from death to life. We do not have to create new things for the giver of life to do. Instead, we trust in the promises of God and give thanks for the Spirit who preserves our faith in spite of sin and doubt.

---

[11]Steven D. Paulson, *Luther's Outlaw God*, vol. 1 (Minneapolis, MN: Fortress Press, 2018), 103.

IN THE HOLY CATHOLIC CHURCH

BRUCE HILLMAN

You are not alone! This is the reality of the church: that God has called out of the world those whom he has made his own and who are united to each other. To confess the reality of the church is to confess the unassailable chasm of sin and death that so separated God from man and men from each other is now intimately bridged. What was once far off and immeasurably hopeless has now been gathered together and lovingly bonded in the very person of Jesus Christ (Heb. 3:6; Col. 1:17–20). To celebrate this work of Christ is to celebrate the harvest; it is to drink the new wine of God's own fruit. For he is the Lord of the harvest, who is himself also, as new man, the first fruits of God's renewing work (Matt. 9:38; 1 Cor. 15:23). To confess the reality of the church is to confess the alienation, loneliness, and hopelessness of the present day, in which all people suffer, to be a thing passing away. The church is a living promise that this "present evil age" has been overcome by the "age to come" and that evil survives only on borrowed time, time that God uses to increase the very harvest for which the church labors (Gal. 1:4; Heb. 6:5; Eph. 1:19–23). The church is the foretaste of the kingdom here and still to come and the place where God distributes his gifts. The church is, in short, a forever-community partnered with Christ. It is the eternal promise that nothing can separate us from the love of God because God and man can never again become separated (Rom. 8:31–39). The church is the joy of union, the security of hope, the witness of grace, and the fellowship of the saints and God. You are not alone if you are in the church.

CALLING OUT AND TOGETHER

"Church" (Greek, *Ecclesia*) has a sense of both being "called out" and "called together." *Klesis*, which makes up the greater word, means, "calling" or "called." When combined into *Ecclesia*, it means "gathered together." But there can be no gathering together unless there is first a calling-out. This calling-out is Christ's work. It draws us out of the world and into himself. Christ calls and brings us life and faith. We are called *out of* and *into*. The church is that community that God has called out of the world, out of death and sin and hell, and into himself and his verdict of grace (1 Peter 2:9–10). But—and this is an essential point—the church is a community called out and into *Christ*. Christ is the head, and without the head, the body cannot survive. There can be no church without Christ, without a cross, without a Spirit (1 Cor. 12:12–27; Rom. 6:3–4). The church, then, is a community, but it is not an independent community. The church is not a fraternity or club; it is not an organization or charity; and it is not an assembly of those gathered around shared beliefs, as if we could ever call a political party or a group of hobbyists who meet together a "church." No. The church is the church because Christ is its head, because he has called it into existence, gathers up its members from the ends of the earth, and sustains and enlivens it by his word and Spirit.

As its head, Christ gives life and direction to the church (Eph. 1:22–23). The community of the church gathers around Christ (the word and sacrament are the only things that give us Christ), and Christ is both the cause and reason for their gathering. But it is a *gathering*. Implicit in the name is the notion of partnership and community. Christ takes the fractured and fragile experiences of humanity, a longing for safety, prosperity, peace, and life, the end of death, and the reunion with loved ones—Christ takes all this—and makes it true.

Only Christ can give the longing of human hearts; only Christ can bring rest to frenzied souls.

The church is gathered by, lives in, and is sustained by Christ. But Christ does not administer his church; he *shepherds* it. When we say he does not administer it, we do not mean he does not have all authority over it or that anything could happen to the church without his consent. Rather, we seek to emphasize *the way* Christ is sovereign and head of the church is by his shepherding care. This care both ensures the destiny of the church but also invites us to participate in God's plan through a relational dynamism. The church, as the hands and feet of Christ's body, serves the Head by making use of its giftedness. Hands grasp, legs run, lungs breathe, and arms wave. To each person, God has given a part to play, to give back, to serve Christ through the body of Christ. Christ shepherds these parts into a unified whole. That is what we mean when we confess the church to be "catholic" or "universal." "Unity" is implicit in "universal," the sense of oneness being the most important aspect comm-*unity*. The body has many parts, but it is only useful as a complete, integrated whole (1 Cor. 12:21–27). The church serves Christ by proclaiming the word of the cross, and in so doing, the church points the world to Christ (Matt. 24:14, 28:19–20; Rev. 14:6; Rom. 10:13–15).

The church's catholicity is not so much its shared doctrines per se as, more fundamentally, its unity around the gospel. The creed unifies but is not the cause of our unification. As such, the church is witness to Christ and his work, for the church proclaims the justification of the sinner through Christ. The hands, feet, heart, lungs, arms, and legs all combine and work together, supporting this witnessing work that both voices and enacts Christ to people. The church has Christ—now, at this moment—but the church also waits for Christ to appear, for the new age to finally shatter the old. This waiting is for the sake of the church's calling and mission. It is a time for proclamation and the heralding of good news. To be with Christ, as the church is, is to be part of his team of proclaimers. You are not alone!

As ambassadors, we find our status only in the fact that we have been called. Christ shepherds his church, drawn out of the world and to himself and then back out again. This going out to the harvest, however, is not a simple return to a former reality. We who were once called out of the world are not simply heading back in, as if our justification was a mere respite from the norm. Rather, this return to the world is one where we are no longer what we formerly were. Baptism and new life constitute a new creation. The sinner returns to the world as a saint, as one no longer under a curse and no longer threatened by death. The Spirit and gifts, Christ and your neighbor, are yours. The return to the world is in many ways a return *for the world* since "you are no longer of the world" (John 17:16). You are not alone!

The church returns as the witness and herald of Christ, who has overcome the world (John 16:33). He has overcome its sin, its death, its alienation, and its continual slide into nothingness. In calling the church to himself, Christ never parts from it, and the church announces God's claim on the world. The existence of the church is a promise from God that the world will live, that the pain and doubt, disease, and death of current experience are to be overwhelmed in the renewing work of the Spirit, and that God has written the ending of the story, which is no end at all. In Christ, the story does not end, for the world, through the mission of the church, gets God. Therefore, the church is privileged and blessed to carry to the world God's gifts, to give it Christ through the word, Spirit, and sacrament.

RECEIVING CHRIST'S GIFTS

Word, Spirit, and sacrament come to us in a formal or objective sense in the Sunday gathering, where we reenact the calling out and the gathered into within the context of worship. Worship too is a gift—a gift that allows us to meet our purposes, for we are most at rest and most alive when we worship. And we worship because God has called us together, and our together-ness consists of receiving and offerings. Those gathered in the church offer back what they have first received. We sing in celebration because God has given us a song. We recite and speak the word because we have received the promises of God. We proclaim the forgiveness of sins because we have received the word of the cross. And we reenact the passion of our Lord because through his passion we have been justified. The church gathers to offer up and give back to God what it has first received because in this response to grace, this living sacrifice that is worship, we are recipients of still more gifts. These gifts do not come because we have offered our praise but because we have been called together by the Lord of the harvest.

That is what the Sunday gathering is. It is the place where Christ meets us to give us gifts. It is the place where offerings are appropriated and returned. In the word, in the sacrament, Christ arrives. He is genuinely and truly present with his people. He is not present in some strange spiritual or metaphorical sense. When Christ says he is present, he does not mean he is symbolically present. When we tell our children, "Don't worry, I'll meet you there at five," we mean what we say. We do not make such promises and then fail to show up and excuse our absence by saying we were only making such a promise symbolically. Christ really comes. In word and sacrament, the Lord who gathers, arrives. The Spirit mediates his coming so that the word and the sacrament unveil themselves, unmasking their appearance with profound comfort—not bread and wine alone, not water only, not words on a page of ancient writing. No! He is here!

He and we, together, become one around him. We are not alone! To receive Christ and his gifts is nothing else than to accept all that Christ does. To receive Christ is to receive the forgiveness of sins, the Spirit of truth, the holiness of righteousness, the life that never dies, the Father who never leaves, the Spirit who quickens us to understanding, the faith that rests on God's words, and the brother and sister next to you who need you, because you bring Christ to them. To receive Christ is to be, eternally and forever, never alone!

"I believe in the holy catholic church." That is, I believe in Christ and all he has done. I believe in the unified and partnered reality of Christ for us, for you, for me. I believe that I am enjoined to an intimate fellowship of Christ's own making that preserves, admonishes, forgives, encourages, proclaims, and strengthens me and to whom I am called to do the same. To give me Christ is to give me you, and me to you, you for me, and me for you, us for the world, us with Christ. We are not alone! The span is overcome and the chasm crossed. We are no longer strangers and aliens. We are Christ's, and he is ours. And the world waits for the church to come, to bring it the very gifts it receives each week. The world waits; it waits for news that death is no more and that evil is condemned. The world waits with longing, even if it is not aware it is waiting, to make the confession that is already in the mouth of the church and that the church claims with grateful and loving confidence: We are not alone!

IN THE COMMUNION OF SAINTS

CHAD BIRD

I deeply appreciate the work of translators, but I wouldn't want to stand in their shoes. Their task is herculean. The words with which they work—nouns and verbs and adjectives and adverbs—are like the threads of a spider web: they're sticky. They're woven into a deeply interconnected language, a single touch of which can make the whole linguistic web tremble.

Because of this, how can a translator fully convey the immense connotations a word has in one language into another? It's like asking a mouse to give birth to an elephant. There's just too much there. One cannot transfer 100 percent of Spanish into English, or Hebrew into German. So translators do the best job they can do. And very often they do exemplary work. But they can't do it perfectly because a "perfect translation" is a logical impossibility. There will be approximations and gaps. And as we shall see momentarily, there will be ambiguities.

Discussing the challenge inherent in translation may seem like an odd way to begin a reflection about "the communion of saints." But not really, because there's a longstanding translational issue lurking behind this creedal phrase. And we must briefly address that issue before we actually talk about what it means.

So first of all, let's make a quick run through English, then Latin, then Greek. Don't worry. It's not as complicated as it sounds. Then, we'll dig down to the Hebrew bedrock of the phrase, followed by a visit to 1 Corinthians and our life in the church today. In the end, I hope that the next time you confess this phrase in the creed, you'll smile a knowing smile, for you'll realize the profound, scripturally saturated gospel truth conveyed in these four little words.

COMMUNION OF HOLY PEOPLE OR HOLY THINGS?

First off, here's a quick summary of the translation issue. Our English phrase "the communion of saints" is from the Latin *sanctorum communionem*. While the English seems fairly straightforward, the Latin is not. It's ambiguous. *Sanctorum communionem* can refer to one of two things: "a communion of holy persons" or "a communion of holy things." Grammatically, the Latin is either a genitive of persons or a genitive of things.

So if the Latin is ambiguous, how do we solve the riddle as to whether "holy persons" or "holy things" is accurate? Here is where the Greek rides to our rescue. The creed almost certainly comes to us from the eastern, Greek-speaking church. As Werner Elert writes, "The whole character of the confession both in style and content demonstrates that it was not derived from the [Latin-speaking] West."[1] And in Greek, unlike the Latin, there is no ambiguity. In its original form, the phrase would have been *ton hagion koinonian*, "communion of holy things." In fact, this language is still echoed in the Greek Orthodox liturgy today when the priest, after the consecration, says, "The holy gifts for the holy people of God." He says this in reference to the bread and wine of the Eucharist. So the "holy things" or "the holy gifts" are from the Lord's altar.

What's the upshot of all this? We usually treat "communion of saints" as a line tacked on to explain further what we mean by the church: "the holy

---

[1]Werner Elert, *Eucharist and Church Fellowship in the First Four Centuries*, trans. Norman E. Nagel (St. Louis, MO: Concordia Publishing House, 1966), 8. See also Herman Sasse, *This Is My Body: Luther's Contention for the Real Presence in the Sacrament of the Altar* (Minneapolis, MN: Augsburg Publishing House, 1959), 389–98.

Christian church, that is, the communion of saints." But here's the problem: *the creed is not defining the church as the communion of saints.* Rather, the creed is confessing that the church is that place where our communion is not in each other ("holy people") but in those holy gifts in which we communally partake ("holy things").

Because the creed in the West has been translated and understood for centuries as meaning "communion *of saints*," it seems we're more or less stuck with that translation. But know this: if we were to confess it according to its origin in the Greek-speaking Eastern church, we would say, "I believe in . . . the communion of holy things." So it's these "holy things" we'll focus on in this chapter.

THE HEBREW BEDROCK

We'll return to the Greek in a moment, but before we do, we need to dig down to the Hebrew foundation of what it means to speak about "holy things" and our participation in them. Why? The Greek language of the creed draws especially upon the Greek language of 1 Corinthians 10, but in that letter, Paul is reflecting a Hebrew understanding of altars, communion in those altars, and the holiness of the sacrifices offered on those altars. Thus, to grasp the full impact of the creed, we need to make a journey to the Torah.

In the Torah, especially Exodus and Leviticus, holiness is not an abstract concept. It's as tangible as blood, as concrete as an altar. We encounter holy space (tabernacle), holy people (Israel), holy clothing (vestments), holy time (Sabbath), and many other holy things (blood, bodies, bread, wine, oil, etc.). None of these are holy in and of themselves but are made holy by the God who is intrinsically and everlastingly holy. He is "Holy, Holy, Holy," as the seraphim sing (Isa. 6:3). Whatever is holy was made or declared holy by God. As Leviticus says repeatedly, "I am Yahweh *who sanctifies*" (20:8; 21:8, 23; 22:9, 16, 32). That is, he is the holy-making, holy-declaring God.

Moreover, God not only sanctifies holy objects but sanctifies people through those holy objects. As John Kleinig writes, "*God communicated his holiness physically with his people through the holy things.*"[2] A person did not become holy by thinking holy thoughts but by tangible participation in holy things. Sanctification happened by touch and taste. For the average Israelite, this happened primarily in sacrifices usually translated

---

[2]John Kleinig, *Leviticus—Concordia Commentary: A Theological Exposition of Sacred Scriptures* (St. Louis, MO: Concordia Publishing House, 2003), 11. Italics in original.

as "peace offerings" (Lev. 3:1–17; 7:15–36). In these sacrifices, the blood of the animal (from cattle, sheep, or goats) was sprinkled on the altar. The fat was burned on the altar, and the meat was divided between the priest and the worshiper. The worshiper, along with his family and others, then cooked this meat and shared it in a sacred, communal meal. They ate the very one whose blood had been shed on their behalf; they consumed the price of their redemption. And this food from the altar made them holy. As Kleinig explains,

> **The main kind of holy food was the meat from the peace offerings (Lev. 19:8). It was the most important item of holy food that was available to the lay Israelites, their way of sharing in God's holiness. Their sacred banquets therefore revolved around the eating of that holy food. Through it they enjoyed holy communion with God.[3]**

The Israelites who ate these sacrifices were sharers in the altar of Yahweh. The holy meat from the holy lamb from the holy altar made holy by the thrice-holy God made them holy. I know, that's a lot of holies, but one cannot underestimate how important this is. Holiness was not earned or derived from their own actions; it

---

[3]Kleinig, *Leviticus*, 11.

was God's gift, put into their mouths. Holiness was something shared by communal participation in a holy meal. They all ate the same Spirit-filled, holiness-permeated food from the altar.

With this Torah understanding of holiness, holy food, and the holy altar, we are now ready to visit 1 Corinthians 10. There we shall see the direct language, based on the Torah, from which we get the creedal phrase "communion of holy things."

KOINONIA IN THE BODY AND BLOOD OF JESUS

The congregation at Corinth was a pastor's nightmare come true. It was riddled with problems, one of which was the temptation of believers to eat meat sacrificed to some of the popular Roman deities of the city.

In chapter 10, the apostle warns his hearers to "flee from idolatry" (v. 14). He asks them to think about this fact: "The cup of blessing that we bless, is it not a participation in the blood of Christ? The bread that we break, is it not a participation in the body of Christ? Because there is one bread, we who are many are one body, for we all partake of the one bread" (vv. 16–17). The Greek word for "participation" is *koinonia*, often translated as "communion" or "sharing." Paul is saying that when we celebrate the Lord's Supper, the cup we bless and the bread we break is a communion in two holy things: the blood of Christ and the body of Christ. When we partake of the table of the Lord (v. 21), we participate, commune, and share in the sacred gifts of God. And this common participation of the many in the one bread unites us into one body (v. 17).

Paul is basing this understanding of *koinonia* on the Torah. As he writes, "Consider the people of Israel: are not those who eat the sacrifices participants in the altar?" (v. 18). When the Israelites ate the peace offerings, they were in communion with the altar of Yahweh, and thus with Yahweh himself. The meat of the lamb or calf or goat, the blood of which had been sprinkled on the altar, joined them to that holy altar on holy ground in front of the holy God. Just as the Israelites could not eat from Yahweh's altar and then belly up to Baal's altar without destroying their own souls by becoming sharers in demons, so the Corinthians could not "partake of the table of the Lord and the table of demons" without dire consequences (v. 21).

Now we finally get to the main point. The Greek word that Paul uses here, *koinonia*, is the same word that is found in the original, Greek phrase in the creed: *ton hagion koinonian*, "communion of holy things." There can be little doubt that there is a straight line from the creed back to 1 Corinthians, just as that line keeps extending all the way back to the Torah. We have *koinonia* in the holy things of God, for we have *koinonia* in the blood of Christ and the body of Christ. We who are many, when we eat and drink from the Lord's table or the Lord's altar, are joined as one body because we communally partake of the same sanctified and sanctifying meal.

Our mouths can confess, "I believe in the communion of holy things" because those same mouths have eaten and drunk of these holy things in holy communion.

THE UNITY OF THE CHURCH IN HOLY THINGS

The church is often described merely as a group of likeminded religious people. They share spiritual relationships with each other. Or, as Herman Sasse writes, the church is envisioned as "a society of pious individuals who formed a fellowship for mutual religious edification."[4]

The Greek original of the creed—not to mention the Torah and 1 Corinthians!—points us in a very different direction. The church is where we participate in a

---

[4]Sasse, *This Is My Body*, 393.

common thing, where we share together the sacred and sanctifying gifts of God. What we have in common, in other words, is outside us, external to us. We commune together in the body and blood of Jesus. And that communion in holy things makes us holy, unites us with Christ and one another, and becomes the way by which we understand what the church is.

The church is the communion of holy things, of the gifts of Christ, specifically his body and blood. In this sacred meal, we eat the Lamb whose blood was shed on the altar of the cross. We drink the very price of our redemption. And as we do, the Father makes us holy, unites us to his Son, and fills us with his Spirit.

Therefore, the next time you confess the creed, think of the profound, scripturally saturated, gospel truth in the phrase "communion of holy things." In this Third Article, we're confessing this:

I believe in the Holy Spirit,
who creates the holy Christian church,
in which we have communion in the holy body
  and blood of Christ,
who gives us the forgiveness of sins in those
  holy gifts,
leading to the resurrection of the body,
and the life everlasting. Amen.

IN THE FORGIVENESS OF SINS

STEVE PAULSON

What an insane idea to forgive sins! For-give means to give *freely*, without measure, as in "before" any payment. Then, more insane yet, this free and unmeasured forgiveness is given for *sin*. That means for-given deals do not happen simply with mishaps or failings, but especially treat the root sin that is unbelief. How do you forgive unbelief? The only solution to unbelief is belief, but doesn't forgiving unbelief just make more unbelief? Furthermore, there is the problem of just how much one forgives. How far does one go to forgive, and how many times does one apply it? The prophet of postmodernity, Jacques Derrida, was once asked to lecture on forgiveness and immediately recognized the problem: there seemed to be no end to forgiveness—no "this far and no farther." This lack of a limit makes the practice irrational and even dangerous. What kind of society can survive on forgiveness, and what kind of Lord would demand it?

Indeed, doesn't free, frequent forgiveness embolden sin? How will the sinner learn, since only pain truly motivates a person to change? Or is it rather the case that forgiveness works on the theory of the carrot rather than the stick? Perhaps forgiveness is simply an act of kindness, and kindness inspires people to change—"paying it forward" with hopes that kindness will boomerang to its originator. But our apostle Paul recognized that even kindness does not attract enemies to your way of thinking but rather heaps hot coals on their heads (Rom. 12:20). That means your acts of kindness are worse than punishment for a man who believes he is innocent and righteous.

PRIDE: OUR DEFENSE AGAINST FORGIVENESS

Nevertheless, Christ taught his disciples to pray this way: "forgive our debts as we also have forgiven our debtors" (Matt. 6:12). By doing so, Christ used both of God's words, command and absolution, to get us to believe in forgiveness. The first defense against forgiveness is pride: I do not need it, and my enemy does not deserve it. So Christ first commands that you forgive. Otherwise you will never do it: "Use this word 'forgive' that I first bestowed upon you, and do not delay." The proud man does not want to forgive or be forgiven but would rather employ the law as God's means of making us righteous. Forget forgiveness. Let us rather do the works of faith! But Christ remains indignant, saying, "Forgive, even though you fear this forgiveness destroys my kingdom and all hope of righteousness." This is why Luther implored, upon the dedication of the first new Lutheran church in Torgau, that nothing else should happen in any church but the preacher saying, "I forgive you," and the congregation saying, "Amen." But what about exhortation and guidance in life and praise and all the other things a liturgy brings? No, the only thing that should happen there is the repeated cornucopia of the gospel's public absolution, the private absolution, the sermon, the baptism, the Lord's Supper, and the mutual consolation and conversation of Christians. Nothing is to be done in this church other than forgiveness.

Christ thought so much of this little word *forgive* that he added his threat: if you do not forgive others, I will not forgive you (Matt. 6:15). That threat is not there to save us but to break a stubborn reed to make us useful as the Spirit's instrument to absolve others. When we believe in forgiveness, we first mean, "I am not so proud that I do not need it, nor will I refuse to give it. It may be a cockamamie idea to give Christ's righteousness to sinners merely by speaking a promise, but if he commands it and even threatens me with it, I'll do it." So, first our pride is removed so that we believe in forgiveness—negatively—and submit to doing the thing: "I don't like it. Forgiveness seems a strange scheme, and I suspect it causes more problems than it mends, but okay, if you want absolution this way—free and merciful, without legal requirement—I'll do it."

BELIEVING THE "FOR ME"

But as hard as it is to believe in forgiveness for others, it is even harder to believe in forgiveness for oneself. Can I believe that with this little word, "On account of Christ I forgive you," some sinful preacher accomplishes belief for me? That would mean with a mere word, my debt of sin is paid, my ransom is given, and through his holy and precious blood, I am freed. It means that the punishment I deserved is taken by the innocent man. Yet it means something even more impossible: my very sins, which I produced, possess, and carry like a heavy weight, are now themselves—wholly and completely—taken by Christ. How he accomplished this feat is too marvelous to behold. His was not a powerful act fulfilling the law where I failed but a purely passive dying by which he took the sins of the world, as John had first preached, "Behold the lamb of God, who takes away the sin of the world" (John 1:29). He took not only the penalty but the sin. He did not simply return me to pre-lapsarian status of Adam and Eve, but he made me new. As Augustine had hoped, I am then unable to sin. That is, Christ's forgiveness of me is the end of the law, and as Paul said, where there is no law, there is no sin to count (Romans 5).

The biggest stumbling block for believing in the forgiveness of sin, however, is not that Christ somehow managed to take the sins of the world upon himself but that in doing so, he also took on my own, particular, concrete, lived, borne, carried, weighty sins. This was Thomas's trouble with believing Christ. He may have believed in resurrection generally, but he could not believe that Christ had forgiven him until he heard it and touched it himself: "Look, my sins are no longer on me, but on Christ! He even let me touch them, and sure enough, those things that were undeniably mine yesterday are his today; not only does he bear them, but he also has done what I could not—he has defeated them once and for all." So it was that Thomas fell down and gave the same confession we give now in our creed: "My Lord and my God! I believe in the forgiveness of sin! I believe in the forgiveness of my own sin."

But why does Christ not give us all a touch of his side as he did Thomas? Because, blessed are you who have not seen but believe (John 20). How are you to believe unless you have heard, and how will you hear without a preacher? Blessed are the feet of those who come over the mountains—the preacher who has arrived to give this greatest of divine gifts to you: I forgive you (Romans 10). When we confess our faith in forgiveness, we confess our faith in Christ's word of promise delivered through a preacher in the present—to me. When we confess the articles of the creed, we are saying out loud and before God's eternal throne that we not only use the means of forgiveness, but we also believe in it. We trust it.

But the greatest temptation comes after we have received this promise and believe it. No sooner do we receive our forgiveness than the devil comes prowling, pointing out that the sins Christ claims to have taken are still hanging on me. Do you not see them with your own eyes and feel them in your heart? If I do not feel them, then my neighbor will obligingly point them out to me: "I see you have a splinter in your eye." This throws me back into disbelief. This was what Paul warned us about in his seventh chapter of Romans: "For I do not do the good I want, but the evil I do not want is what I keep on doing. . . . Wretched man that I am! Who will deliver me from this body of death." (Rom. 7:19, 24) The sins Christ told me were forgiven are not only still present, like a bag of maggots around my neck, but active. They speak more loudly to me than the promise of forgiveness: wretched man that I am! What am I to do with Christ saying: "I forgive you," in one ear, and my sins saying, "Here I am, there is no change," in the other?

OUR NEED OF DEATH

Faith is no easy matter. Indeed, it is impossible for humans. Worse yet, faith comes only at the expense of terror, trial, and torment. Belief in forgiveness must come from outside, specifically from the Holy Spirit, because faith believes in a thing not seen. Forgiveness is not only invisible to our eyes, but God also actively hides it from us. But forgiveness has even more working against it than its hiddenness. God hides it so we do not deal with it in the way we deal with everything else in our lives, which is to count, measure, gauge, and trust the law as God's one, final will. The insanity and impossibility of believing in forgiveness is that here God is doing his own special, unique, divine will in its proper (not alien) sense. God is not only a giver (the first article of the creed) but a for-giver. He gives already in creation without our worthiness, but he forgives entirely apart from the law. This is what makes salvation different than creation, the old world different than the new creation, and forgiveness not merely a surprising act of release, but a divine attack on sin and the sinner.

When God forgives, we do not remain more or less like we were before—only without guilt or charge. We are put to death. God's forgiveness is not a wink and nod, a "let's do better next time," or mere return to "go." The attack is not only upon the individual sinner but upon all who are complicit in this sin—including the devil, the world, and our sinful flesh—but also upon God's own holy law. Confessing belief in the forgiveness of sins is the end result of a great cosmic battle pitched by God, through his Son in the Holy Spirit, by which he overcomes our great foes: sin, death, wrath, devil, and even God's good and holy law.

When we look upon ourselves, especially our external appendages or members (as Paul calls them), we see nothing but sin and naturally say, "This forgiveness cannot be. I see and feel that sins are still mine, and I must bear them." But Christ speaks differently: "Come you who are heavy laden, and I will give you rest." Christ tells us to take his light yoke, while he takes our heavy one (Matthew 11). Belief in forgiveness teaches us to pray against our selves—against our feeling of sin. Here, Luther says, ignore sin! Talk back to it, and say, "You are no longer mine. You belong to Christ!"

So it is that belief in forgiveness of sins is a mighty, fighting faith that opposes all contrary words with this one little phrase: *I forgive you*. No other word belongs in your conscience, and when the law comes and says, "Now give this to others," you say, "I need nothing to make me more righteous, and yet I will not despise giving this word of forgiveness, which is life and salvation not only to me but to many. Indeed, not only do I gladly take up this office, but it has already been done without your saying so. I trust the Holy Spirit is making use of me and this word, even without my praying or worrying. How many times shall I forgive? At least as many times as I have been forgiven, and this is technically innumerable." In this way I confess, "I believe in the forgiveness of sins, despite its insanity, and I forgive others as I have been forgiven."

IN THE RESURRECTION OF THE BODY AND LIFE EVERLASTING

KELSI KLEMBARA

As the words of the Apostles' Creed etch into my memory over time, they simultaneously fade from the forefront of my mind and heart. This is more of a gift than one might expect, because it is a gift that ensures the words of this ancient confession stand outside of my disposition, my uncertainties, and my fears while still binding me to Christ's bride. So I recite them and go about my Sunday and my week, just as easily as I wash my hair and feed my dog every morning. But then something in life happens—a disruption (small or large) takes place, suffering surprises me out of nowhere, or grief sets in—and these words no longer feel as commonplace. Their meaning once again catches me off guard—perhaps because I doubt them, because I am too angry to believe, because I find myself with nothing else to hold onto, or a mixture of the three.

I find myself in this disruption right now. It's been just over a month since I miscarried, since I felt the hope growing in my body turn to grief. It's been just over a month since my unborn daughter left this world before she entered it. Yet as I wrestle with these 109 words and the Scripture that supports them, I can't help but find comfort. In its conclusion, the Apostles' Creed reminds me that Christ's resurrection means the reversal of things as we know them, and in doing so, this proclamation turns my attention back to what I hold to be true. As Luther confidently states, "If we are satisfied with the creed and the doctrine, what does it matter even if hell and all the devils fall upon us?"[1] And so it is in distress, and even in disbelief, that we continue to profess these words, hoping against hope that they remain true (Rom. 4:18).

THESE BODIES OF DEATH

"I believe in the resurrection of the body and life everlasting. Amen." So ends the confession of faith I share with the rest of the universal church. For the world, this is surely a bizarre phrase, eliciting images of zombies or

---

[1]Theodore G. Tappert, *Luther: Letters of Spiritual Counsel* (Vancouver, BC: Regent College Publishing, 2003), 98.

illogical wishes. If I had to guess, most of us, no matter our belief system, would probably choose to ditch our tired, worn-out, failing bodies as quickly as possible rather than seeing them raised to new life.

Our bodies serve as a constant reminder of the law, regardless of how much or how little we realize it. Even before we were obsessed with our weight, our health, our hair color, or our cuticles, no man or woman escaped the realization that their flesh was leading them straight to the grave. Our bodies are the vehicles of our certain demise; they are, as Paul says, "bodies of death" (Rom. 7:24). They groan and creak and sometimes scream at us that everything is not the way it should be. They demand our perfection while being unable to accomplish it, and thus they literally embody the sin and the law we leave undone. "The heart beats violently and feels nothing but the pressing burden of sin and fear of death, so that it must cry out," says Luther.[2]

Death is the end of us. It's the end of everything we know and love. It rips those we are closest to from us before we are ready. It comes on its own time and in its own way. It tells us that all of our attempts in life didn't matter, and all of our successes were fleeting. Death is the decaying, rotting truth none of us can escape. It's no

---

[2] *Luther's Works*, 28:118.

wonder we fear it with such fervor. It's no surprise each of us does everything humanly possible to convince ourselves that we're different, and *our* bodies won't give out on us.

As a reflection of the law, we tend to either worship our bodies or work to escape them (and sometimes, we even combine the two). The fitness movement, self-love movement, and transhumanism movement are just a few examples that all share one common goal: to trade the condemnation of death for salvation by turning the body into some sort of receptacle of righteousness. No matter the approach, whether our bodies are elevated as idols or ignored as sources of pain, it seems we're looking for salvation in all the wrong places.

Early Gnostics certainly had this same problem. Suspicious of earthly, material things, Christian Gnostics in the first century refused to accept a salvation based on the bodily resurrection of the God-man and the hope for the future resurrection of Christians. Instead, they believed it was the spirit, or soul, that was both the way to salvation as well as the only part of humanity worth saving. The Gnostics hoped to escape the physical world to be saved by the spiritual.

THE GLORY OF GOD'S SCARS

Yet God reveals that pitting the physical against the spiritual is not the way he works. Instead, he claims all of it. He is the Creator of heaven *and* earth, conceived of the Holy Spirit *and* born of a virgin Mary. He is fully God *and* fully man—coming to earth in bodily, incarnated form. He lived, suffered, and died, just like the rest of us, and yet, he rose again, as the first fruits of the coming resurrection for those who believe in him (1 Cor. 15:20). And as we await his return, he chooses simple, physical means—water, wine, and bread—to redeem us. We need not dualistically choose between the physical or the spiritual. Both matter to our heavenly Father, and both are promised to us in the life to come. As Luther says:

> **The body is not to be distinguished from the soul, as we customarily do when we hear the words spirit or spiritual. No, we must understand this to mean that the body, too, must become spirit, or live spiritually. We have already begun to do that through Baptism, by virtue of which we live spiritually with regard to the soul and God also views and regards the body as spiritual.[3]**

---

[3]Ibid., 28:192.

Even in his glorified state, Christ's hands and sides still show the scars of the cross (John 20:27). But why? Why would the perfected and transformed Savior still carry these marks? Perhaps to serve as a reminder of the way he works as well as who he is.

Without the physical and historical Jesus, the problem of sin and death, and therefore the problem of our broken bodies, would still need solving. "God himself had to enter the world of real sin in order to bear the responsibility of real sin," says Kazoh Kitamori.[4] It's through Christ's body, beaten and broken and then raised to new life for us, that the enemies of this life and the next are defeated so we might obtain the gifts of resurrection and everlasting life. While our sin continues to distract us with salvation attempts that avoid all suffering, we witness Christ willingly taking on suffering, to the point of death itself. "The last enemy to be destroyed is death" (1 Cor. 15:26), and in defeating the grave, Christ promises that we, too, will rise again.

The cross counters all earthly attempts at justification. It's here that Christ saves through suffering and weakness rather than victory and strength. It's here that Christ chooses to redeem the "lowliness" of the fleshly body. And yet, at the cross, Christ conquers what we

---

[4]Kazoh Kitamori, *Theology of the Pain of God* (Eugene, OR: Wipf & Stock Publishers, 1965), 35.

cannot and redeems what we would rather worship. The scars on his hands become a sign of his victory, a part of his perfection, for by his wounds we have been healed (1 Peter 2:24). As a result, we hope in the promises he has given us, that God is a God not of the dead but of the living (Mark 12:27). Only by putting our trust in Christ can we lay down our confidence in our earthly bodies subjected to sin in exchange for hope in life everlasting.

HOPE IN GOD'S PROMISES

Even in this hope, the Apostles' Creed echoes the apostle Paul by reminding us that knowing the exact details of the resurrection of the body are not necessary: "But someone will ask, 'How are the dead raised? With what kind of body do they come?' You foolish person! What you sow does not come to life unless it dies" (1 Cor. 15:35–36). We don't need to fill in the blanks of the resurrection with our own, best-imagined details. In fact, we shouldn't even try. Scripture, as summarized by the Apostles' Creed, tells us that our future hope falls outside of the realm of how we wish things would be, because this realm still resides within the sin and imperfection of this life. We can loosen our grip on the hope we have in what we think should be or could have been because God's promises outweigh even the best of our wishes. "If the life to come would not be different from what reason conceives it to be, I, too, would not wish for it. However, how things will be must be judged not by our reason but by God's Word," Luther reminds us.[5]

What I want is my daughter here and now. I want to see her smile for the first time, to see her take her first steps, hug her when she's sad, and cheer her on when she succeeds. Yet I trust that she is now with her heavenly Father, as I will be one day, and that this reality will be better than what I could possibly fathom. This does not minimize sorrow and heartbreak in this life, but God's promises do free us to grieve hopefully for ourselves and all of God's children. He has told us already that we can trust that at Christ's second coming, our bodies will be glorified (Phil. 3:21), transformed from the earthly to the heavenly (1 Cor. 15:46), and given eternal, everlasting life (Matt. 25:46, John 11:25–26). God promises to give us so much more than the here and now in the eternity to come, for "the former things shall not be remembered or come into mind . . . no more shall be heard in it the sound of weeping and the cry of distress" (Isa. 65:17, 19).

---

[5]*Luther's Works*, 28:172.

LIFE EVERLASTING

Life everlasting follows the resurrection of the body as the consummation of God's promises. This final stanza reminds the Christian of the Creator's promise to renew us to life without end, without judgment, and without defeat. Through Christ, the power of death and the devil have already been silenced (Heb. 2:14). We can trust this is true, even when our experience tells us otherwise. Death has lost its sting (1 Cor. 15:55–56), and the dead in Christ will rise again to be with the Lord forever (1 Thess. 4:15–17). Life everlasting is the final nail in death's coffin, and with death's death, all the power of sin to keep us from God Almighty also dies.

Life everlasting will be pure, gospel life where we will no longer "labor in vain or bear children in calamity" (Isa. 65:23) but where God will dwell with his people (Rev. 21:3). It's this future we hope in as we wait for the resurrection and glorification of our earthly bodies and the release from bondage for all creation (Rom. 8:31). The biblical narrative begins with creation in the garden and ends with creation through a renewed heaven and earth, a sure promise that the Creator cares for all of his creation, even you.

"I believe in the resurrection of the body and life everlasting." What a good and true promise this simple sentence is for the addict, the anorexic, the mentally and physically disabled, the terminally ill, and all of us who march one step closer to death each day. What a good and true promise this is for me—and my husband—and for all families who grieve the loss of the smallest ones. What a good and true promise for those who weep at the loss of the saints who have gone before them. No matter our circumstances, the redeemed in Christ are comforted to know that one day death will cease to reign, and we will be reunited in the physical and everlasting arms of our Savior.

With these final words of good news, the Apostles' Creed ends in amen. The amen echoes the words of Paul in 2 Corinthians 1:18–20:

> **As surely as God is faithful, our word to you has not been Yes and No. For the Son of God, Jesus Christ, whom we proclaimed among you, Silvanus and Timothy and I, was not Yes and No, but in him it is always Yes. For all the promises of God find their Yes in him. That is why it is through him that we utter our Amen to God for his glory.**

In the amen, our belief is confirmed as being in agreement with the promises given to us in God's word. We believe in a God who does what he says he will do. From the beginning, he has been the God who keeps his promises as, time and again, he works to save, preserve, and gift his people. As God's people, we join together to profess our Creator is three in one. It's on account of his death and resurrection that we can proclaim the good news of the forgiveness of sins, the resurrection of the body, and life everlasting. The defeat is over, and the Victor has already been named. It's in this hope that, during the quiet moments as well as the worst disruptions, we continue to proclaim aloud that Christ is risen and soon—very soon—he is coming back again.

CPSIA information can be obtained
at www.ICGtesting.com
Printed in the USA
FSHW010832021019

9 781945 978784